MOULE'S

PATENT EARTH CLOSETS

AND COMMODES.

"It (the Conference) asks for the *abolition of all privies, with cesspools or wells, and the substitution for them of movable receptacles, such as* EARTH CLOSETS *or* 'FOSSES MOBILES,' *which can be frequently emptied and cleaned, and which may be so arranged that fæcal matter cannot soak into the soil.* The contents should be carried out of the towns. The Conference objects to the system of drains or sewers in communication with houses, holding that in practice we cannot prevent the diffusion of noxious gases through the houses in connection with them, and that in times of cholera drains may spread the disease along a line of houses in communication with them; and that, owing to the porosity and rapid decay of masonry work, they readily allow of the impregnation and saturation of the ground through which they run with decomposing organic matters. When used, sewers should never be allowed to empty themselves into rivers, and waterclosets should never be within the houses themselves."

MOULE'S PATENT EARTH CLOSET CO., LIMITED.
NO. 29, BEDFORD STREET, STRAND, W.C.

THOS. M. EVANS,
General Manager and Secretary.

H. J. AND J. W. GIRDLESTONE, 31, DUKE STREET, WESTMINSTER,
ENGINEERS TO THE COMPANY.

PRICE LIST.

The Cottage Commode, in Plain Deal, Unvarnished, with
"Pull-Up" Apparatus £2 5 0
Commode in Plain Deal Case, Varnished, with "Pull-
Up" Apparatus 3 10 0
The same, Extra Size and Make 4 10 0
Commode in Plain Deal Case, Varnished, with Self-Acting
Apparatus 4 0 0
The same with Fixed Seat 4 10 0
Commode in Oak or Mahogany, French Polished, and
on Castors, with "Pull-Up" Apparatus . . 6 10 0
Commode in Oak or Mahogany, French Polished, and
on Castors, with Self-Acting Apparatus and Fixed
Seat 7 0 0

The Self-acting Mahogany Commode is also made in a smaller size,
especially for night use.

All the above are furnished with Pails. Extra Pails without Covers,
4*s*. 6*d*. each. With Covers, 5*s*. 6*d*. each. Sieves, 4*s*. 6*d*. each.
Glazed Enamel Pails, extra.

The APPARATUSES for placing in FIXED or EXISTING CLOSETS are
sold separately, as follows :—

The "Pull-Up" Varieties, with Handle, Pan, &c. . £1 10 0
The "Self-Acting" Varieties, with Seat and Pan . . 1 15 0

*** Packing Cases and Wrappers will, *in all cases*, be charged ; but
half-price will be allowed on their return, free of carriage.

When any number of Commodes or Apparatuses are required, a
special arrangement can be made.

*** *The following Works, relating to the Earth System, are on Sale at the Office :—*

	s.	*d.*
NATIONAL HEALTH AND WEALTH. By the Rev. H. Moule	0	6
THE SEWAGE OF TOWNS. Papers by Various Authors, read at the Leamington Congress	3	6
MATTER AND EARTH. By Dr. Hawksley	2	6

MOULE'S
PATENT EARTH CLOSETS.

THIS invention effectually remedies evils arising from the common cesspool privies and water-closets when the drainage is defective, and the supply of water imperfect; and it effectually prevents the offensive smell consequent on the use of the ordinary commode in Bedrooms, Hospital Wards, Prison Cells, &c.

It is founded upon the well-known power of earth as a deodorising agent: a *given quantity* of earth destroying all smell, and entirely preventing noxious vapours and other discomforts. The practical application of this power has been successfully carried out by the present invention, which treats all the operations *in detail*.

Apart from its superiority over the water system in destroying all smell, the earth system is more economical, both in the first cost and its after-working; there being no expensive cistern or pipes; no danger from frost; and the product being a manure of value to farmers and gardeners. The supply of the earth, and its removal, are attended with no more inconvenience than the supply of coal and the removal of ashes, whilst the value of the manure amply pays the cost. Added to which, the sifted ashes, instead of lying in the dustbin until they become a nuisance, may be mixed with the earth, and thus lessen the quantity required.

THE PRINCIPLE OF THE EARTH CLOSET

consists in an apparatus for measuring and delivering the requisite quantity of earth, and in a reservoir for containing it. This apparatus can be applied to most existing closets.

AN ORDINARY FIXED CLOSET

requires the apparatus to be placed at the back of and in connection with the usual seat, the reservoir for containing the earth being placed above it. Under it there should be a chamber or vault, about four feet by three wide, and from two to two and a half feet deep, with a paved or asphalted bottom, and the sides lined with cement. Should there be an existing cesspool it may be altered to the above dimensions. Into this the deposit and earth fall, and may remain there three, six, or twelve months, and continue perfectly inodorous and innoxious, merely requiring to be occasionally levelled by a rake or hoe. If, however, it should be found impossible or inconvenient to have a vault underneath, a movable iron trough on wheels may be substituted. In this case it will be advisable to raise the seat somewhat above the floor, to allow the trough to be of sufficient size.

By one form of construction, (the " Pull-Up,") the pulling up a handle releases a sufficient quantity of earth, which falls into the pit or vault, covering the deposit, and completely preventing all smell. By another, (the " Self-Acting,") the same effect is produced by the action of the seat. The apparatus may be placed in and adapted to almost any existing closet or privy, and so arranged that the supply and removal of earth may be carried on inside or outside as desired.

The apparatus is sold separately, and may easily be adapted or fixed by any carpenter. A lithographic drawing with instructions are sent with each ; or, on receipt of a sketch, with dimensions of the place in which it is intended to fix the Closet, full directions will be given for fitting the machinery, which may be had with or without the necessary woodwork.

DESIGNS FOR FIXED CLOSETS.

The following designs are intended to show how the apparatus is

FIG. I.—PLAN FOR SINGLE CLOSET.

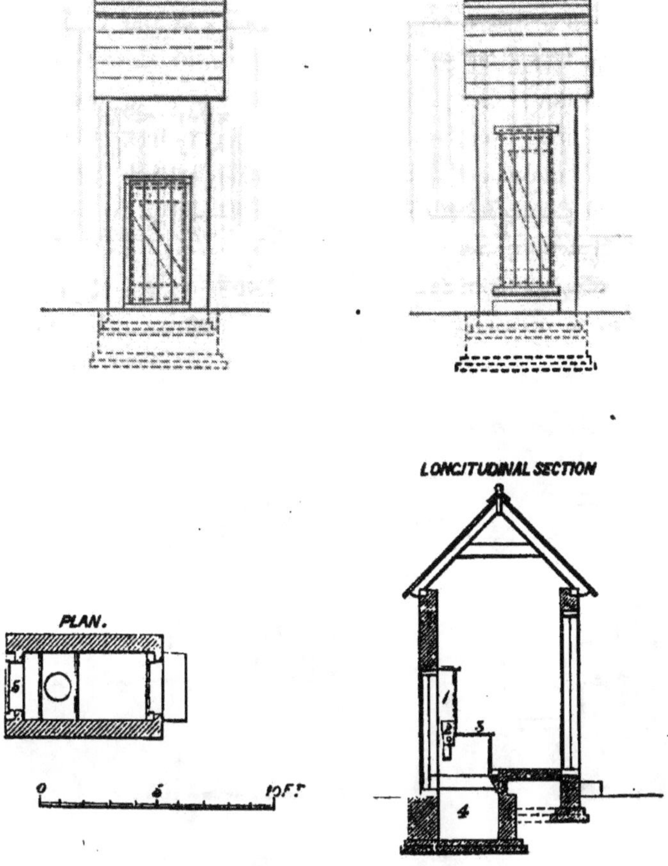

1. Earth-box.　　　2. Hopper.　　　3. Seat.　　　4. Vault.
5. Door at back to enable Earth-box to be filled, and Vault emptied. This door is not
necessary when the Earth-box is filled and the Vault emptied from the inside.

adaptable to privies, either single, or in sets of one, two, or six. They
are so simple as to require no further explanation; and working plans
for them or for others extended to sixteen or twenty closets, may be

FIG. II.—PLAN FOR FIXED CLOSETS IN A SET OF TWO.

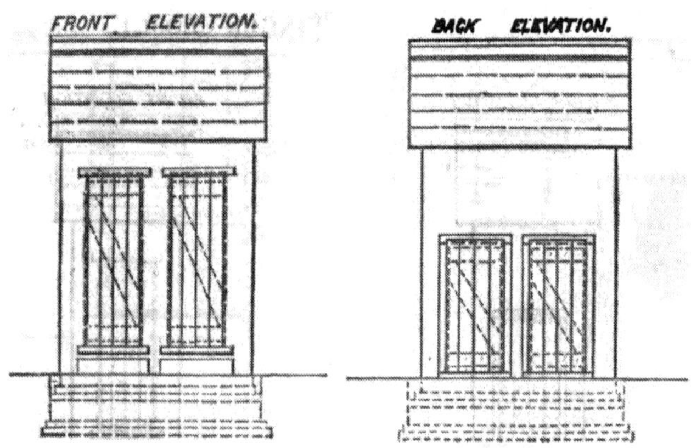

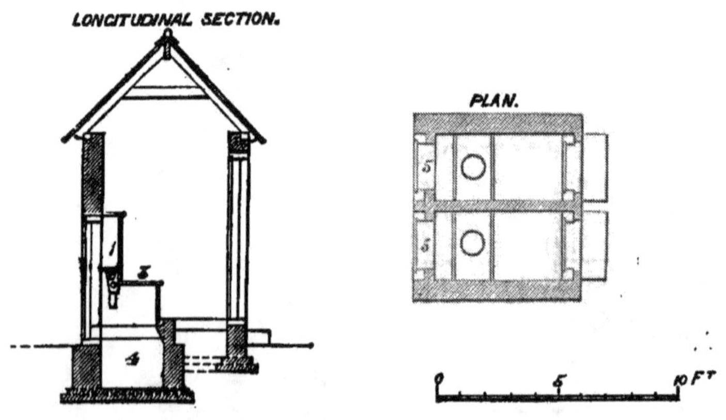

1. Earth-box.   2. Hopper.   3. Seat.   4. Vault.
5. Door at back to enable Earth-box to be filled, and Vault emptied. This door is not
necessary when the Earth-box is filled and the Vault emptied from the inside.

had from the Company. Of course, the form of building may be altered at pleasure, and the same mechanical arrangement may be adopted in existing privies.

FIG. III.—PLAN FOR FIXED CLOSETS IN A SET OF SIX.

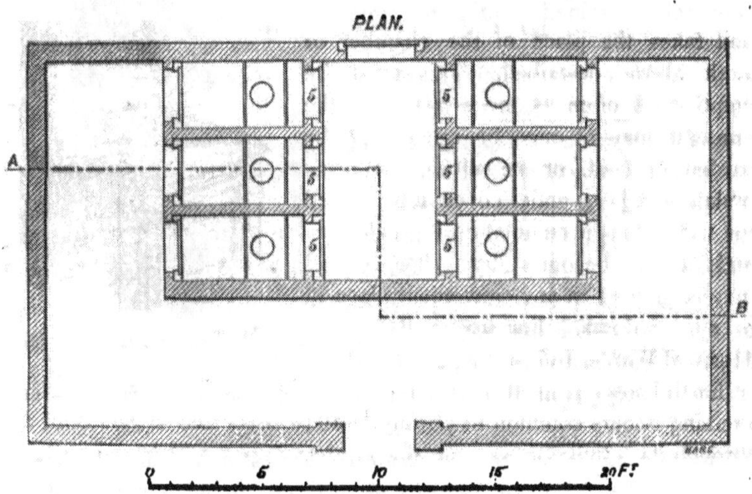

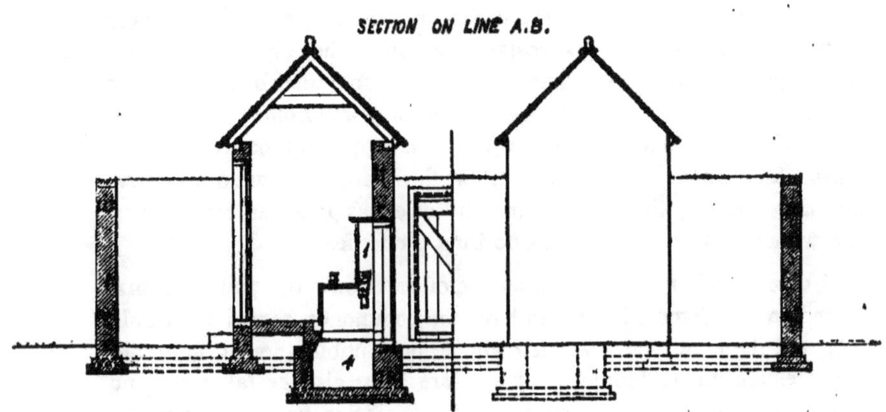

1. Earth-box.　　2. Hopper.　　3. Seat.　　4. Vault.
5. Door at back to enable Earth-box to be filled, and Vault emptied. This door is not necessary when the Earth-box is filled, and the Vault emptied from the inside.

THE PORTABLE CLOSET OR COMMODE.

In the Portable form of Earth Closet, (see fig. IV.) the apparatus and earth-reservoir are self contained, and a movable pail takes the place of the chamber or vault above described. This must be emptied as often as necessary, and the contents may at once be applied to the garden or field, or bè allowed to accumulate in a heap under cover until wanted for use. This accumulation is inodorous, and rapidly becomes dry. The Closet may be placed in any convenient place in or out of doors. For use in Bedrooms, Hospital Wards, Infirmaries, &c., this form

Fig. IV.—Commode, 1·11 wide, 2·2 deep.

of Earth Closet is invaluable. It is entirely free from those faint, depressing odours common to portable water-closets and night-stools, and through its admission one ot the greatest miseries of human life, the foul smells of the sick room, and one of the most frequent means of communicating infection, may be entirely prevented.

These Closets are made in a variety of patterns, from the Cottage Commode, to the more expensive ones in mahogany or oak, and vary in price accordingly. They are made to act either by a handle, as in the ordinary water-closet, or self-acting, on rising from the seat. The Earth Reservoir is calculated to hold enough for about twenty-five times; and where earth is scarce, or the manure required of extraordinary strength, the product may be dried as many as seven times, and without losing any of its deodorising properties.

If care be taken to cast one service of earth into the pail when first placed in the Commode, and to have the commonest regard to cleanliness, not the least offensive smell will be perceptible, though the receptacle remain unemptied for weeks. Care must also be taken that no liquid but that which they are intended to receive be thrown into the pails.

DIRECTIONS FOR USE.

The first requirement for the proper working of the Earth Closet is earth perfectly dry and sifted.

Earth alone is proved to be the best deodoriser; and by experiments lately made by Dr. Fawcus under the direction of Dr. Mouat, Inspector-General of Gaols in India, far superior to any disinfectants; but where it is difficult to obtain earth abundantly, sifted ashes, as before stated, may be mixed with it in proportion of two of earth to one of ashes.

As the first requirement is *Dry Earth sifted*, and as this is usually thought to be a great difficulty in the way of the adoption of the Dry Earth System, the following remarks will at once remove such an impression.

The Earth Commode and Closet if used by Six persons daily will

FIG. V.

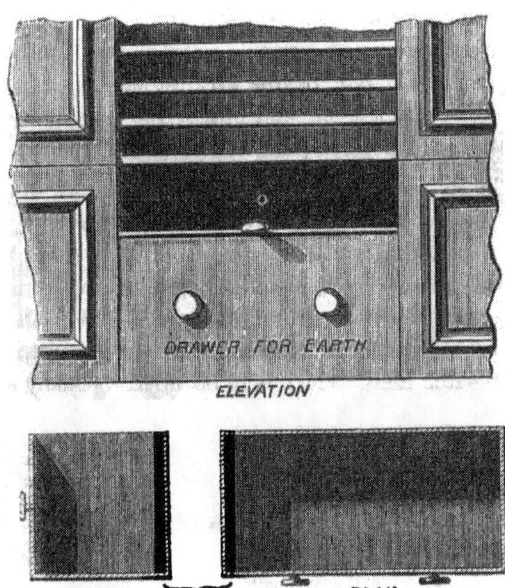

require on an average one bushel or one hundred weight of earth per week. This may be dried for family use by a contrivance shown in fig. v., which represents a drawer made to fit under the kitchen range, and which is to be filled with earth one morning and left until the next. The drawer should reach to within two inches of the bottom bar of the grate.

Fig. vi.

A frame, with a handle, covered with fine wire netting, forming a kind of shovel, should be placed on this drawer ; the finer ashes will fall through, mixing with the earth, whilst the cinders will remain on the top, to be from time to time thrown on the fire. The laundry stove, hot plate, or oven after baking, may also be applied to drying earth.

The consumption of earth for One Hundred people would be less than a ton per week.   In this case a dryer (fig. vii.), made of bricks and sheet iron, may be erected in any covered shed or building.   The one figured

FIG. VII.—THE CRAWLEY DRYER.

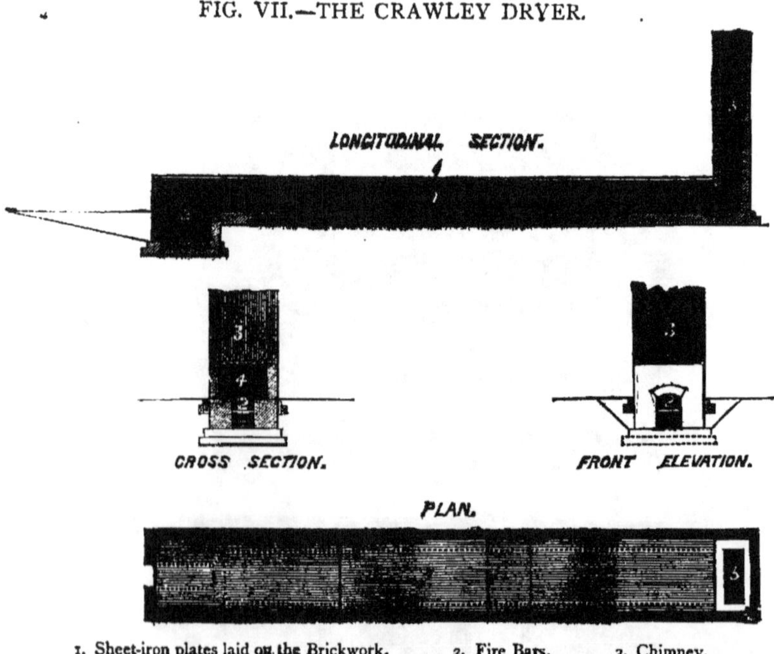

1. Sheet-iron plates laid on the Brickwork.   2. Fire Bars.   3. Chimney.
4. Hot-Air Chamber.

will dry nearly three tons in a day and a night, and the cost of the fuel—small coal and coke mixed—will not exceed 1s. 6d. per ton.   It may be made larger or smaller according to the requirement. This furnace is fixed, and applicable for Barracks, Unions, Mills, Infirmaries, Hospitals, Asylums, Gaols, &c. A plan for building it may be had on application at the office. The necessary sifting is easily effected by means of a riddle, three feet square, and similar to those used in sifting wheat.

Should, however, a fixed dryer be found inconvenient or impracticable, the movable one (fig. VIII.) may be adopted, and will dry a large quantity daily, with very trifling cost for fuel. The same earth may be dried and used four or five times if desired, with the same deodorising effect, the product increasing in value. As the product is perfectly inodorous, it may be removed at any time without offence to smell or sight.

But a more economical method is to provide in the summer time a winter store of dry earth, which may be kept in a hot-house, shed, or other convenient place, just as we lay in a winter store of coals.

FIG. VIII.

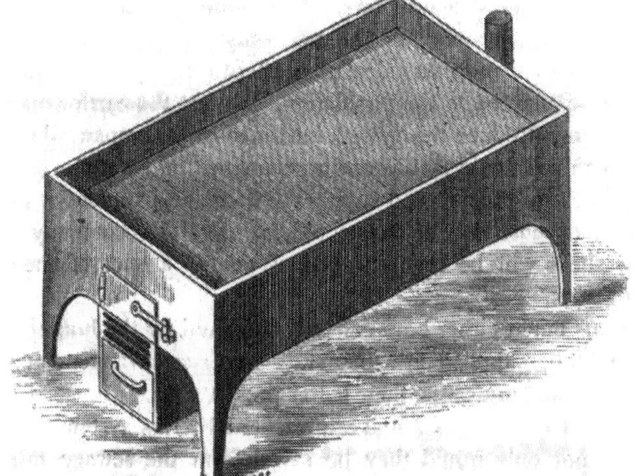

PORTABLE DRYER.

APPLICATION OF THE DRY EARTH SYSTEM TO TOWNS, VILLAGES, AND OTHER LARGE COMMUNITIES.

As in the case of Private Families, or of Larger Establishments, the first requirement is a sufficient supply of dry earth; so in the application of the earth system to Towns or Villages, this is the first thing to be considered.

A population of 10,000 would require from sixteen to eighteen tons of earth per day; the return for which in increased bulk would be from twenty to twenty-four tons. As, however, the earth is only required as a loan, there can be no difficulty in procuring the necessary quantity; particularly as the earth borrowed is only worth earth price, whilst that returned is worth manure price.

As the fixed drying apparatus, figured on page 10, may be extended to any size, there is no difficulty here. It becomes simply a question of outlay, in the first instance, for the necessary sheds and drying apparatus; and of horse and cart calculation afterwards. Just as the waterworks must be adapted to the population, so must the earth-works.

In order to introduce the system into a town a company should be formed, which will be in fact a manure company, and which will find it to its advantage to prepare and supply the earth, and remove it at least without any expense to the householders. For this company drying and store sheds will be requisite, and of course a staff of men with horses and carts.

The closets might either be purchased and fixed by the householders, or they might be supplied at a moderate rent; an arrangement which might ensure, in many cases, their better preservation.

To the rate-payers the advantages presented by this system are great indeed, for not only would they be saved from the sewage rate, but from all expenses arising from broken pipes, stopped-up drains, and all their attendant discomforts.*

---

* The annexed calculation, made by a disinterested person for the city of Chichester, may be regarded as an approximation to the cost of working the Dry Earth system, but the value of the product is nearer £3 per ton than 15*s.*

"A population of 8000 would involve the importation of fourteen and a quarter tons of earth. In big places products would be five and three-quarter tons, making in all

It is of course impossible in a Prospectus to go much into detail, but this Company would be ready to co-operate with local authorities, and to

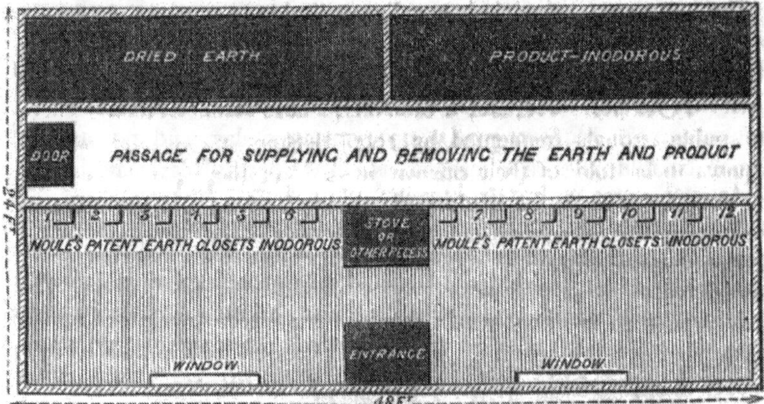

FIG. IX.—DESIGN FOR A PUBLIC CABINET.

treat liberally with corporate bodies or individual projectors and contractors. Particular attention is requested to the Statement and Testimonials annexed :—

twenty tons to be exported from the city. Assuming that four vans, with two horses each, and attended by two men each, would be sufficient for this purpose, the probable working cost may be taken as follows :—

		£	s.	d.
14¼ tons of earth, bought at 7s. per ton		4	19	9
8 horses' maintenance, at 3s. 6d. per day		1	8	0
8 men.......................3s. 6d. ,, ...		1	8	0
4 vans wear and tear ......5s. 0d. ,, ...		1	0	0
2 horses for use at kiln ...3s. 6d. ,, ...		0	7	0
2 carts wear and tear ......1s. 6d. ,, ...		0	3	0
2 men at kiln ....3s. 6d. ,, ...		0	7	0
Incidental expenses per day		0	7	3
Per day		10	0	0

This would amount to £3650 per year. The produce would be twenty tons of manure per day, which, taken at 15s. per ton, would yield £15 per day, or £5475 per year, (or at £2 per ton, £14,600), leaving a surplus of £1825 (or £10,950), which would do more than pay for drying, kiln, horses, vans, carts and other appliances the first year, and afterwards leave £1500 or £1800 (or in the greater proportion) per annum clear profit. But I feel quite sure I have over-stated the cost of earth and working expenses, and understated the value of the product."—*West Sussex Gazette.*

URINALS.

The DRY EARTH principle is equally applicable to URINALS, especially *for schools and railway stations, and other public places.* Self-Acting machinery for these urinals is supplied by the Company, and all offensive smell may be prevented, and a valuable manure manufactured. There are public urinals frequented by 2000 persons a day, and no one requires to be told of their offensiveness. Yet these places may, by the use of dry earth, be made perfectly inoffensive ; and the value of the manure that is now wasted, but which then would be saved, would be highly remunerative.

FIG. X.—DESIGN FOR URINAL.

*** *The following letter from Mr. James, of Halton, to Mr. Board-man, of Norwich, is reprinted, without any comment.*

HALTON, TRING,

25th *January*, 1867.

DEAR SIR,

I am sorry that my other engagements have prevented me from answering your letter of inquiry before.   I am not surprised to find that Boards of Health hesitate to adopt Mr. Moule's method of deodorizing and utilizing town sewage, for the promise which is held out to them, of easy application, at small cost, dims the prospect of success, which is in reality as certain as the application ; but I am astonished to find that some of your neighbours have tried this method and found it a failure. There must have been a want of common precaution, which has never had place here ; for, as I told the Congress at Leamington, of all the foul smells which once afflicted this village, none remain at this moment.

Some gentlemen, you say, complain of the dust—for myself, I have never been incommoded by it ; but it is as certain that dry earth will be dusty as it is that water must be damp, and I fancy as little inconvenience will arise from the one as from the other.   The commode, with its attendant pail, is only adapted for a sick room.   For that purpose it is one of the greatest luxuries ever invented, and no gentleman's house should be without one.   My experience confirms my first impression, that the use of the pail, as advocated by Dr. Hawksley, and, I see, by you also, is a very great mistake—the greatest mistake, in fact, which anyone advocating the earth method can fall into.   The nuisance and trouble of the daily removal of deposits would be quite intolerable to a household—insupportable in expense, and perfectly unnecessary as a sanitary measure.   With rare exceptions, present arrangements may be adapted to the new system, and the periods for cleansing the cesspits would depend entirely upon their size and the requirements of the household they are intended to serve.   The deposit may be allowed to remain for any number of years without the smallest annoyance to any one—the only precaution necessary being the exclusion of all liquid except that which comes from the human body.

I have had no opportunity as yet of getting any personal experience of the value of the earth manure; but in the spring various dressings will be made on different crops with earth passed once, twice, thrice, and four times through the closets. When the result has been ascertained, I shall be pleased to communicate it to you.

What your engineer tells you about Manchester is perfectly true —it does cost them some thousands to get rid of the sewage, which they very sensibly decline to cast into the river; but the system adopted there is as much like Moule's method as Greek is like Coptic. Seventy-seven thousand privies are cleansed annually, and the only dry stuff applied to the deposits is the fire ash, in quantities wholly insufficient to absorb the urine or to deodorize the soil. Taken in this condition from the cesspits it is unfit for immediate application to the land, and so it is transported by railway to distant soils, where the farmer has to do for it at great cost and trouble, what might be done more profitably on the spot, by the continuous application of dry earth. The situation of your city, in the midst of a turnip growing country, differs materially from that of Manchester, where the land is cropped with tall chimneys instead of grain. In Manchester, the condition in which the deposits are when taken from the cesspits, renders its immediate transport from the neighbourhood a matter of necessity, but towns using the dry earth method may (pending a sale) store their manure in the very centre of the population without any inconvenience.

It is perfectly true that the feeling of the *real* Congress at Leamington was decidedly in favour of the dry earth method, and it is equally true that the resolution which was carried was in favour of the wet one. I will explain what I mean. The town of Leamington has sought, by means of sewers, to cleanse itself, and promote the health of the inhabitants, at the expense of the health and comfort of the Earl of Warwick. Litigation followed, and the town's people were beaten and exasperated. A local surgeon, a strong advocate of the dry method, summoned a Congress to consider the question of sewage generally, and at the close of the discussion the room was crowded by those who had taken no part in it, and had not heard one word of anything which had been said. But I for one consider that, although engineers and their friends interested in costly irrigation or filtration works, either finished or in course of construction, assembled in great force, it was very manifest that the largest proportion of those who took a real part in the Congress were in favour of the dry earth method.

Personally, I know nothing of what was done at Aldershott, but from what I have heard I am induced to believe that the loss sustained by the Government must be regarded as another instance of War Office mismanagement.

If you gentlemen at Norwich do make up your minds to give Moule's method a fair trial, I should recommend you to have nothing to do with any professional man. A committee of gentlemen interested in the experiment, with the aid of a journeyman carpenter to fit the closets, and a labourer of ordinary intelligence, will constitute all the scientific force required. You must observe that the cost of an experiment in irrigation is told by thousands, whilst the earth method may be fairly tried, at a very small cost, in any chosen spot.

The River Pollution Commission has given the public the result of their investigations, and they strongly recommend that the irrigation system, as practised at Croydon, should be the plan generally adopted throughout the country, for preserving the health regardless of the pockets of the people. The prospects held out by this commission (of which an engineer, be it observed, is at the head) are so very cheerful, that every one liable to pay a rate to a Board of Health ought to read it. They wholly condemn the many experiments which have been made to disinfect or filter—both, they say, have been costly failures. They report that there is no reason to suppose that irrigation by sewage is prejudicial to health ; although one doctor at Norwood had intimated to them that a new form of ague which had recently made its appearance there, might be attributed to the vicinity of these works. The works, they admit, *may* depreciate the value of property in the neighbourhood. They say that experience has shown it to be necessary that the land to be irrigated should be the property of the Town, and they recommend that Boards should be allowed to purchase one acre for every 50 people (1,500 acres only for Norwich !). When this has been purchased, and the sewers constructed in the costly method inflicted by science, you have the source of all disease still festering and stinking in the midst of your population. It is the dweller down stream only who has been benefited. The principle which the " dry earth people " seek to establish is, that everyone should be compelled himself to abate the nuisance he creates ; and there is no reason why the fluid should be treated in a different manner to the smoke nuisance.

The course of cropping is rye grass, produced in vast quantities, and then follows the exhaustion of the ground by means of root crops, to prepare for further doses of sewage. What effect the constant repetition of this system may have, either on the productive qualities of the land, or the health of the neighbourhood, it is not possible to say; but there are eminent medical men who tell us that cattle fed on the grass thus produced are liable to filthy conditions of the body, which they, in their turn, will contribute to those who eat their flesh. The Commissioners observe upon certain neglects of precaution which will entail "*unpleasant, if not mischievous, consequences,*" and that the "model works of Croydon" occasionally send off the water either turbid or so "*imperfectly cleansed from sewage that it pollutes both the river Wandle and the atmosphere in the vicinity;*" but all this, they say, admits of explanation. "*Sewage irrigation,*" they tell us, "*requires to be conducted with strict attention; the site must not be too near to dwellings; adjoining wells must be watched.*" Expense, of course, is no object anywhere! "*Sewage can be pumped any height and carried to any distance. Its conveyance, therefore, to any point is merely a matter of cost.*" The irrigation system requires, it seems, scientific application, the costly services of an able professional, and a vast expenditure of money; and for these reasons it is rising to be one of the great institutions and monster nuisances of this engineer-ridden country.

Fortified by these *strong* recommendations, the advocates of irrigation assembled at Leamington in full force ; the process they recommended was simple and *not* so very costly after all. Talk of smells ! whoever heard of such things at Croydon ? No one—for the Croydon people, with a regard for their own health and comfort which they don't exercise towards their neighbours, have (the Commissioners tell us) established their irrigation three miles from their Town. It was hinted that the sewage fields might be made into pleasant promenades ; and it was broadly stated that the principal drains were the favourite haunts for trout. Here is an opportunity for a people's park ! ! But, strange to say, the Commission which had heard all this recommends—What ? That the land to be irrigated shall be one mile from the Town, and should lie to the North or East of it. Why ? because such spots are, and always will be, destructive to the value of adjoining property, prejudicial to health, and a nuisance to everyone in the neighbourhood.

Yours faithfully,

J. JAMES.

To MR. EDWARD BOARDMAN, ARCHITECT,
    NORWICH.

TESTIMONIALS.

As new inventions are generally received with more or less mistrust, attention is invited to the following Testimonials.

From Captain Armytage, Governor of the West Riding Prison, Wakefield.

WEST RIDING PRISON, WAKEFIELD, Feb. 4, 1867.

SIX months having expired since the Visiting Justices of this prison granted authority for bringing "Moule's Earth Closets" into use, I have great pleasure in bearing testimony to the value of the earth system. We have 800 cells without water-closets, and we are about placing Earth Closets in them. We have now 100 of the latter in use. I have not had a single complaint from either warders or prisoners since we commenced using the Earth Closets. The Earth Closet cells are without the smell that commonly exists in the water-closet cells.

The supply of dry earth is given weekly, or when required, the closet containing at the back (with care) a sufficient supply for fourteen days ; however, to be quite secure, the pans are emptied, and a fresh supply of earth given once a week without the slightest smell in the building during the time of removal.

We have taken the precaution to make the Earth Closets self-acting; this leaves nothing to be done by the prisoners that can disarrange the apparatus. We have established a small kiln for drying the earth, and can always keep up a good supply. The earth, after being used in the closets, is turned over, and pulverised once a week during the first three weeks, when it is quite fit for the farmer or gardener. No smell arises from working the soil, and in time I anticipate a profitable return for the first outlay. I shall during the coming year be enabled to observe the effect of the manure on the crops grown within the prison.

Where the closets are in use, we have been able to do without the deodorising powder used formerly, and during the late hard frosts we were obliged to place the earth closets in cells already supplied with water closets, the pipes being frozen. Our plumber is much in favour of the earth closets ; he strongly recommends that in future they should be placed in all parts of the prison in lieu of the water-closets (an opinion certainly against his own interests).

G. ARMYTAGE, Captain,
Governor.

From Dr. Hawksley.   To the " Times."

BROOK STREET, GROSVENOR SQUARE, Sept. 13, 1866.

BEING on a visit in the country, I was invited to inspect a small infirmary for the sick poor on the estate of the proprietor.   In all respects its arrangements appeared to me excellent, but especially in the fact that it possessed no water-closet.   In place thereof I found an earth closet, which in appearance, method of using, comfort, and convenience, was the counterpart of an ordinary good water-closet, with the difference that each use of the handle supplied the pail beneath with a certain quantity of dry earth, which perfectly absorbed and deodorised whatever material had been cast into it.   The attendant in charge assured me that its use had been most salutary, agreeable, and convenient.   At suitable times the pail was taken to a distance, and its contents buried in a pit for manure.   The dry earth was supplied through a hopper above and behind the closet, and worked easily with each movement of an ordinary closet handle.

THOMAS HAWKSLEY.

From J. James, Esq., Halton, Tring.   To the " Times."

Sept. 17, 1866.

THE process of deodorisation by earth, referred to in Mr. Hawksley's letter in the "Times" of Friday last, may be seen in full operation on Baron Rothschild's estate here.

Any one taking an interest in the improvement of the condition of the poor, and the state of our rivers, would do well to satisfy himself of the truth of Mr. Hawksley's views by a personal inspection of the whole process.

In the earth sheds here he may see excrementitious matter on its first removal from the closets, and in barrels, dried and ready for the corn and turnip drills.   In all its stages it is perfectly inodorous, even when subjected to the fiercest summer heat.

The deodorisation may be effected either by the rough and ready application of a shovel-full of garden earth every day, or by the more refined and very effective apparatus patented by the Rev. H. Moule.   It is with this little machine that the Halton closets are fitted ; they are cheap, self-acting, and cannot get out of repair.

To the benefit conferred by them on the poor, the cottagers themselves will speak. There are yet enough of the old cesspools remaining to enable a visitor to appreciate at a glance the perfection of the Earth Closet system.

I can see no reason why this method should not be adopted in towns.   It is inexpensive and most efficacious, requiring no better engineer than a journeyman carpenter.   The earth may be taken in at long intervals and stored like coals, while the cesspools might remain unemptied for three, six, or twelve months, according to their size or the convenience of the tenant, without causing the smallest annoyance.

With rare exceptions, existing water-closets and cesspools are available for the earth method, and are readily adapted at a very trifling expense.

J. JAMES.

From G. Faithorn, Amersham.   To the " Times."

Sept. 20, 1866.

AT this critical time, when we are in momentary danger of outbreaks of cholera at our doors, I thought it desirable not to lose a moment in accepting the challenge offered by Mr. James in his letter in the " Times " of yesterday, and I rode across the hills to Halton this morning for the purpose of investigating the truth of the assertion he had made.

I inspected the earth sheds and saw the process in every stage.   I put my nostrils into close contact with soil which had been taken from the closets this morning, and I took up some which had been out no more than a fortnight without soiling my hands, and lastly, I have come away with a small parcel of the dried soil in my pocket, having during the whole investigation met with nothing in the smallest degree disagreeable. I have no hesitation in saying that any gentleman who follows the example of Baron Rothschild in adapting this process to cottages will confer the greatest possible boon upon the poor, and I shall myself have no hesitation in recommending not only the process itself, but the little machine invented by Mr. Moule, to any one seeking my advice.

In small towns, at least, it must be of easy and inexpensive application, while the benefit to health will be great indeed.

GEO. FAITHORN,
Medical Officer of the Chesham District of the
Amersham Union.

Extract from Report by Dr. Mouat, Inspector-General of Gaols in India.

IT is, in my humble judgment, impossible to over-estimate the benefits that will result from the labours of the Rev. Mr. Moule in this important branch of hygiene— the dry-earth system.   It has already, in the infancy of its introduction in Bengal, worked wonders, and I have little doubt that its economic advantage will hereafter be as great as its immediate influence in promoting the comfort and improving the health of all public institutions in which it is properly used. . . . The papers printed in the appendix show that the dry-earth system of the Rev. Mr. Moule has been attended with success ; that it has removed the greatest defect in the sanitary arrangements of Indian prisons ; that it has led to a remarkable change in the condition of such extremely unhealthy gaols as Monghyr and Gya, and that it is without exception the greatest public benefit conferred by a private individual in a matter so essential to public health that I am acquainted with.

Extract from the Report of the Select Committee on Night Soil, Melbourne. Ordered to be printed (May 10, 1866) by the Legislative Council.

AFTER a careful investigation, your Committee have arrived at the conclusion that earth is a perfect deodoriser,   . . .   and that closets so constructed as to ensure its proper application are free from all objections which attach to cesspools and water-closets. No noxious exhalation arises from their use, or on the removal of the contents, and the chief obstacle to the drainage of the city, &c., is consequently removed.

Your Committee desire to urge the general adoption of earth closets. They serve a twofold purpose; (1) By their use either in public institutions or private dwellings, immunity from noxious exhalations and the filtration of poisonous fluids through the soil may be secured; (2) Also a very valuable fertilizing agent may be obtained.

Your Committee have ascertained that earth closets can be fitted up . . . and kept in order . . . at less cost than cesspools could be constructed and cleansed.

Mr. Moule's earth closets are those in use in Melbourne, the patent being worked there by his permission.

From J. Smedley, Esq.

MATLOCK BANK HYDROPATHIC ESTABLISHMENT, RIBER CASTLE, MATLOCK; AND LEA MILLS, NEAR DERBY.

May 31, 1866.

GENTLEMEN,—I find your patent Earth Closet a perfect success. It may be used in any room without the slightest effluvium being perceived.

J. SMEDLEY.

From the Secretary of the National Rifle Association.

NATIONAL RIFLE ASSOCIATION,
12, PALL MALL EAST, *August* 12, 1865.

GENTLEMEN,—I am directed by the Council of the National Rifle Association to express to you their thanks for having placed at their disposal during the Wimbledon Meeting several of your Patent Commodes. I am further directed to state that they proved to be of the greatest use, and were found to act admirably.

EDW. ST. JOHN MILDMAY, Sec. N. R. A.

From Oswald Foster, Esq., Hitchin.

HITCHIN, *March* 19, 1866.

GENTLEMEN,—Your Earth Closets have been in use for two years in the sick wards at the Hitchin Union house. As medical officer at that establishment I can speak with the greatest confidence of the vast convenience and comfort they have been to the inmates, indeed, to all connected with the institution, as, since their introduction, the annoyance and evil of disgusting effluvia attendant upon the use of the old-fashioned commodes have been avoided. The prejudice in the minds of many, not only amongst the poor but the more educated, at the introduction of anything new is patent to most; but I feel sure that any attempt to return to the old commode would create great dissatisfaction amongst the occupants of our sick wards.

OSWALD FOSTER, Surgeon.

From John Wilson, Esq., Edington Mains.

Hitherto, we regret to say, that the numerous and costly attempts that have been made to separate the fertilising matter from the water in which it is contained, have proved utter failures. The most feasible plan for the utilisation of nightsoil is that brought forward by the Rev. HENRY MOULE, of Fordington Vicarage, Dorset.

From John G. Talbot, Esq.

NEW FALCONHURST, EDEN BRIDGE, KENT,
May 4, 1866.

I have very great pleasure in bearing my testimony to the great value of the Earth system, as carried out according to the Rev. H. MOULE's invention.

I have had personal opportunities of testing the system, having set up several apparatus about the house, stables, and garden. I have also strongly recommended its adoption by the Board of Guardians of which I am an *ex-officio* member, and by the Contractors of the Surrey and Sussex Railway, which is about to pass through this place.

The wonderful effect of the system in removing the great nuisance of bad smells, which are almost inseparable from the ordinary privies, as well as the great value of the manure which the Earth system renders perfectly inoffensive, makes it a matter of surprise that the arrangement is not universally adopted.

I shall have great pleasure in recommending this system to any one who may be influenced by my opinion.

JOHN G. TALBOT,

From the Rev. H. B. Miles.

BURLESTON RECTORY, DORCHESTER,
January 29, 1866.

GENTLEMEN,—Some months ago, having constant trouble with my water-closet, which was very much out of repair, I determined to make a trial of the dry-earth system in its place. I have now in constant use one of your *self-acting* Earth-Closets, and my purpose in writing is to express my perfect satisfaction with it in every respect. It occupies the place of the old closet up-stairs, the soil falling into an enclosed space beneath, about five feet square, reaching to the ground-floor, and with a small door opening into the yard, from whence, about once a month, it is removed without the least offence. The trouble of carrying the dry earth up-stairs I consider to be about equal to the pumping water into the cistern under the old plan. I have used the same earth four or five times without the least inconvenience, and have now a quantity of valuable manure for my garden. I do not think we can estimate the immense advantage a general application of this system would prove, not only in our towns and cities, but in the country at large.

HENRY B. MILES.

Extract from Mr. Simon's "Memorandum on Disinfection."

PRIVY COUNCIL OFFICE, *July*, 1866.

"In country places, where proper drainage is not provided, the nuisance of open privies may be best avoided by the use of the so-called Earth Closet."

Dorset County School, Dorchester.

February 11th, 1867.

Having been requested to give my opinion as to the working of the Patent Earth Closets which have been in use for the last fifteen months in the County School, I beg leave to state the following particulars.

We resolved to try the Earth Closets in consequence of the water-closets getting continually out of order. As a matter of course, offensive smells as often arose, and we had reason to believe that a severe sickness which befell us was mainly to be attributed to this fact. I am thankful to state that since the introduction of these Earth Closets we have been free from both offensive smells and sickness. One very great advantage in them is, that it is hardly possible for them to get out of repair; at any rate ours have cost us nothing as yet, nor are they likely to do so, whilst, on the other hand, under the old system, the cost for repairs for two years amounted to more than £4.

It is, perhaps, well to add that there is nothing offensive to the sight or the smell in the removal of the earth from the premises. On one occasion, when some quantity was being removed in open day, three medical men of this town gave testimony that they could discover nothing offensive.

R. G. WATSON, M.A.

From the Rev. J. W. Neat.

WYKE HOUSE, NEAR WEYMOUTH, *February 12th*, 1867.

Mr. Moule having requested me to send you my opinion of the Patent Earth Closet invented by him, I can safely say that it is a great improvement upon the old plan of out-of-door vaults, and in-door water-closets, there being no smell, no derangement of water-pipes by frost, &c., and, moreover, the Earth Closet furnishes the best manure of the garden.

I lately used one of the Portable Earth Commodes for a sick-room. It was there for a week, in repeated daily use, and not emptied till the end of the week ; there was no smell during all the time. I so entirely approve of the plan that I am now having the out-of-door places altered into Earth Closets for my pupils. You can make what use you like of this note.

J. W. NEAT.

MOULE'S PATENT EARTH CLOSET COMPANY LIMITED,
29, BEDFORD ST., STRAND.